W9-ABV-091

# PORTFOLIO 6

# METROPOLITAN SEMINARS IN ART

## Portfolio 6 · *Composition*

### by John Canaday

ART EDITOR AND CRITIC
THE NEW YORK TIMES

# THE METROPOLITAN MUSEUM OF ART

© 1958 by The Metropolitan Museum of Art

Printed in U.S.A.

# COMPOSITION

## Pictures as Structures

IF ANY painting is the most famous in the world it is Leonardo da Vinci's *The Last Supper* (Plate 61).

*The Last Supper* is a great picture with a religious subject. That is not exactly the same thing as saying that *The Last Supper* is a great religious picture, which it is not. In any mystical sense, at least, it is not a religious picture except by the association of ideas. Nor did Leonardo intend it to be one. In all reverence he conceived of the moment when Christ says to his disciples, "One of you shall betray me," as a moment of unparalleled human drama. It was the psychological atmosphere of that moment that fascinated Leonardo, and he directed every element of his composition toward its expression.

The drama as he conceived it is an interplay of three states of mind and spirit: that of Christ, who makes his announcement with foreknowledge that the events leading to his crucifixion are in motion; that of the faithful disciples, who are filled with confusion, astonishment, and incredulity; and finally, that of Judas, who has already made the bargain of betrayal. The expression of the total atmosphere of this moment, of the three contrasting psychological states made into a unified whole, is achieved through composition. Every element is studied in itself, but each takes on its full meaning only in relation to the rest of the picture. Leonardo apparently sought to reveal the individual state of mind of each disciple. To that end he first studied each man as a per-

sonality, drawing on what facts were known and what legends and surmises there were about him; then he invented for each one a set of features he thought to be characteristic; and finally after long study he gave each one gestures and facial expressions that would complete the psychological description.

Now plenty of other pictures have been constructed just as carefully as *The Last Supper*, but it would be hard to find another in which the construction is so clear and simple, yet so unobtrusive and expressive. Let us insist that the composition of *The Last Supper* does much more than hold together a picture of great size. *It is an expressive factor in itself.* As a matter of fact, the facial types and expressions that Leonardo developed with such care are now so blurred that they are all but indecipherable and the original color harmonies have faded, thus modifying the psychological effect Leonardo intended them to have. Yet the picture still says what Leonardo wanted it to say because the over-all composition remains clear.

*The Last Supper* is painted across the full width of the upper end wall of a long room, originally a refectory. The simple one point perspective of the painting continues the lines of the actual architecture of the room itself. More importantly, though, these perspective lines are a concealed compositional device. A diagram shows that, continued, these lines converge at the head of Christ, or, if you prefer, they radiate from his head like rays of

Photo by Anderson

*Figure 1*

light (*Figure 1*). These lines are united by an arc, formed by the upper molding of a pedimented window above Christ's head. This arc, the only curved line in the architecture of the painting, is a segment of an invisible circle whose center is the same point at which the perspective lines converge. There are other relationships: two of the lines, those that follow the molding along the ceiling, pass through the ends of the arc, and the edge of the circle opposite the arc just touches the horizontal line of the table.

When we say that this invisible circle, with its center at the head of Christ, is like a halo we do not mean to suggest that Leonardo had any such symbolism in mind. He has rather pointedly omitted the halos customary in paintings of the Last Supper, thus emphasizing the human drama rather than the divine mystery of his subject. But the fact that this circular form, the only one in the picture, does surround the figure of Christ tends to set him apart much as a halo would have done. Even if Leonardo had had any such idea in mind he did not intend that the observer should have to do this kind of detective work to notice it, any more than he meant that we should consciously follow the continuations of the perspective lines to Christ's head. He meant these lines to do their work, structurally and psychologically, as part of the total effect of the painting. And they do so, whether or not we are aware of them.

It might seem that once we have detected some of the devices the painter has used to create his drama, the drama itself might be rendered less affecting. This would be true if *The Last Supper* were nothing more than a kind of card trick. Once a trick is explained it has no further interest, since its only function is to puzzle us. But *The Last Supper* is not a card trick; it is a great painting. We may simultaneously enjoy its effect and the means that Leonardo has used to achieve this effect, just as we may be moved by great music and at the same time admire the musician's technique and be aware of the composer's inventiveness.

6

Photo by Anderson

*Figure 2*

Our second diagram shows us that the figure of Christ as it appears above the table is triangular in shape and closely integrated with the lines of the architecture (*Figure 2*). There could not be a more appropriate form: the triangle is the simplest, the most stable, and yet, with its apex, the most climactic of geometrical forms. This triangle, as a final, logical, and harmonious statement, is approximately equilateral. Its lines may be continued into the perspective lines of the floor pattern to form a larger triangle of the same proportions.

It is worth noticing that while the figure of Christ is closely integrated with the basic architectural scheme—the structural foundation of the picture—the figures of the disciples are not. This is one of several devices that not only draw attention to the figure of Christ but isolate him psychologically in this particular moment of his life. Thus unified with the static architectural forms, Christ's figure is invested with divine calm that contrasts with the human agitation of the disciples.

The disciples are divided into four groups of three each. The two groups on either side of Christ echo the central triangle without repeating it exactly. The groups at the ends of the table also repeat the triangle but echo it more faintly, as is indicated in our second diagram. If these groups were as purely triangular as the central figure they would tend to compete with it. But as it is they come to a climax in the figure of Christ: vaguely formed at the far sides of the picture, more definitely formed on either side of Christ, they culminate in the purely formed triangle of Christ himself.

This is part of a scheme to build the picture in a current of excitement that moves toward the center, where it reaches its greatest intensity, and there breaks against the serenity of the central figure like waves against a rock. Thus, Christ is again set off, in his noble acceptance, from the weaker human excitement surrounding him. An accelerating movement runs through the disciples, along their arms and the folds of drapery, growing more violent as it approaches the center, where it is turned back by an uplifted hand on the right and, on the left, by the figure of John "the beloved disciple," who turns away in grief.

In most paintings of the Last Supper John the Beloved is shown leaning toward or on Christ and being comforted by him, but Leonardo abandons this convention to isolate Christ in this moment at the beginning of the trial, conviction, and execution that he must bear alone. Leonardo also departed from convention in putting Judas among the other disciples instead of by himself on the other side of the table. For Leonardo's conception of the Last Supper, Judas would then have been made too conspicuous. As it is, he appears, clutching his bag of silver, in the group to Christ's right, the only one of the disciples who is not protesting the statement of betrayal that Christ has just made.

This outline analysis of *The Last Supper*'s composition could be enlarged to include any detail of it. For instance, the play of Christ's head against the light of the window constitutes the strongest light-and-dark contrast in the picture. The hangings on the wall, because they diminish in perspective, are a series of vertical lines growing closer and closer together as they approach the center, just as the action of the figures grows quicker and quicker as it moves toward Christ. There are subtleties of balance at every turn. In the major one Christ's head is bowed slightly off center to our right. Why? There are two reasons. The obvious one is that as an attitude it is expressive. But the head could have been bowed forward instead of to one side and been just as expressive. If it had, though, there would have been no relief to what would then have been a too rigid and obvious symmetry. The slight bending toward the right supplies the necessary relief. But it also creates a new problem. Such a variation in so conspicuous a spot must be countered elsewhere if it is not to throw the scheme too strongly to the right. Hence, Leonardo's emphasis on the chief secondary figures, Judas and John the Beloved, on our left.

Think, then, how much is involved in a factor as small as the bending of a head: rigidity and monotony are avoided and a place is made for a narrative comment (on Judas) that would not otherwise have been balanced, since there is no incident of comparable importance to put on the other side of the picture—and yet we are aware only that Christ's head is bowed in an appropriately expressive way.

The beauty of *The Last Supper* as a composition is that it is original without being eccentric, highly calculated without being complicated. In it pictorial structure and intellectual conception are consummately unified.

## A Compositional Failure

As a contrast to the unity of *The Last Supper*, since a failure can be as illuminating as a success, Raphael's *Transfiguration* (Plate 62) is one of the most confusing compositions in the world. It is impossible to tell exactly where in the group of excitedly gesturing figures in the lower half we are being asked to look. The eye is told to move in a dozen directions at once. No sooner does it begin to follow any one of the emphatically indicated routes along a pointing arm and finger than it is peremptorily checked and told to follow another. Figures point this way and look that; first we are crowded off to one side, then swung across to the other; we see a patch of landscape in the distance but are denied access to it. If we escape into the upper half, we are in an area of forms so obvious, so much weaker than those below, that our interest is not held, and we re-enter the jangling confusion that we have just left. An attempt to diagram the composition would result in an incomprehensible and irrational web of lines stretching arbitrarily from point to point. Something like a warped triangle with the ascending Christ at its apex would emerge, but the only figure that really holds its own in all this confusion is the kneeling woman who dominates the foreground and, indeed, the whole picture (*Figure 3*).

Photo by Anderson

*Figure 3*

This figure is beautiful in itself in spite of the strained artificiality of attitude, but this beauty is not sufficient reason for the figure's prominence. As far as the miracles (Matthew 17:1-8, 14-18) represented in the painting are concerned the figure is only an accessory, with no more significance than most of the others and with less than some. Its importance should have been given to the epileptic boy to the right, whose miraculous cure by Jesus so astonished the onlookers. In a sound, if obvious, bit of composition the woman points to the boy, but her gesture is nullified by the stronger line of her glance in the opposite direction. In short, the composition fails because it lacks unity and focus. The spasmodic crisscross, the abrupt turns and interruptions, could have served effectively to express the excitement and agitation of the moment if they had been organized toward an appropriate climax, but as it is they only confuse the observer and obscure the narrative.

It may be argued that to compare this composition with *The Last Supper* is unfair since Leonardo's subject was a quieter one involving only thirteen figures instead of twenty-seven. But this is not so; the problem only seems simpler because the solution is presented with such clarity that it appears to be inevitable. For the sake of argument, however, *The Transfiguration* can be compared, still to its disadvantage, with an even more complicated, even more violent subject that involves even more figures, Poussin's *The Rape of the Sabine Women* (Plate 63).

As in *The Last Supper*, but used toward a different end, literally every detail, no matter how small, is integrated within the whole of *The Rape of the Sabine Women*. The composition is built upon a triple framework. First, there is the strong diagonal movement upward from right to left stated by the nude warrior in the right foreground, a linear continuation of the figure of the old man grappling with him. It is repeated in the middle distance by a rearing white horse, in the foreground center by the back of the crouching old woman, and at the upper left by the staff held by the red-robed figure. A dozen other repetitions are discoverable at a glance.

Second, this surging movement is counterbalanced by one in the opposite direction; some of the elements of this upward movement from left to right are the uplifted folds of the red robe, the raised arms of two women who struggle against their abductors, two swords in the background, the fleeing figures that move out of the picture at the far right, and, again, many others. These two systems overlap; most of the figures and groups carry elements of both. For instance, the white horse is integrated with the first system, while the woman

9

*Figure 4*

who is being carried away on his back is part of the second. Her captor is part of a third system, which is a stabilizing repetition of horizontals and verticals. They are most apparent in the lines of the architecture. Also, the red-robed figure stands vertically, there are strong horizontals in the clouds, and verticals or horizontals in various arms, legs, and draperies, and in small details everywhere.

Upon this skeleton Poussin has constructed a composition in which there are various elements that can be better understood when we reach the end of this discussion. We will look at *The Rape of the Sabine Woman* once more at that time, returning now to the point at which we left our discussion of *The Last Supper*.

## Triangular Compositions

When Leonardo used a triangle as the central element in *The Last Supper*, he was capitalizing on the most popular geometric form in painting. A picture planned for some conspicuous central position in a building often demands a symmetrical composition that builds up to a climax at the center—when we have said that we have just about demanded the triangular form. This was so true during the Italian Renaissance, when altarpieces were the painter's stock-in-trade, that the triangular composition crystallized into a formula. The altar itself is the climax of the symmetrical structure of a church. Everything leads inevitably to it, and thus, to the altarpiece. To cap the architectural scheme with a painting that would throw it off balance is unthinkable. The balance was usually achieved by symmetry. Perugino's *Crucifixion with Saints* (Plate 64) is such a pure application of the triangular formula that it could have been designed to illustrate it.

Let us say immediately that the altarpiece is the kind of picture that suffers most by removal from its original location to a museum. Today religious paintings seen lined up by the dozen along museum walls grow monotonous and sometimes we feel guilty that they do. But we need not feel guilty; we are quite right: installed in this way they are monotonous.

Many pictures, particularly modern ones, are painted with museum exhibition in mind. Each one is designed to compete for attention by its individuality. Each diverts us; each offers newer and more curious forms and combinations of color, like dust jackets in a bookstore. But an altarpiece never had and was never supposed to have the appeal of competitive novelty. Each one was painted to be seen by itself, not as part of a gathering of exhibition pieces. It was meant to be seen, frequently by candlelight, as part of the ensemble of a church or chapel.

Nor was the altarpiece created in the knowledge that it would become one element in a collection of historical specimens mounted for critical observation. That is exactly what most of them have become, and this is, of course, exactly the way we are treating our Perugino when we discuss its composition. But in doing so we should try to remember that it is an altarpiece—particularly vulnerable when it is not seen as it was intended to be seen, as part and climax of a certain architectural scheme and a certain emotional atmosphere.

The formula for the triangular composition, repeated dozens of times in Crucifixions, Nativities, Madonnas with Saints, and similar subjects, calls for a central triangle with the picture's focal point at its apex and a secondary, weaker, inverted triangle to counter it. In his *Crucifixion with Saints* Perugino uses the formula with particular grace. There is additional interest in that it unites three separate panels. Saint Jerome, in the left panel (*Figure 4*), forms one side of the triangle with the "line" of his upward glance directed toward the head of Christ. This line exists as strongly as if it were actually visible, like the dotted lines in comic strips that lead from the eye of a character to the object he is looking at. It not only forms a side of the triangle but unites the left panel with the center one by cutting

*Figure 5*

11

Owned by the artist, on extended loan at the Museum of Modern Art, New York

*Figure 6*

across the dividing frame. The body of Saint Jerome bends forward from the waist at the same angle.

In the right panel the Magdalene creates a similar line (*Figure 5*). Her body is not bent, but her head is tilted in the same direction as the line of her gaze toward the apex of the triangle. The forms of the rocks just behind her strengthen the line by echoing it, as does the fold of her robe from ankle to hip. The figure of Saint John, at the right of the cross in the central panel, directs the eye to the apex in the same way. The Madonna, however, looks downward. (How repetitious and obvious it would be if she also looked upward.) But the head of Christ, bowed as if it were looking in her direction, suggests the missing line. The Madonna's bent head supplies a slight but necessary variety among the four figures at the foot of the cross and serves to single her out as most important.

The counter triangle is determined primarily by the landscape on either side of the cross. It is also repeated in folds in the drapery of each figure and by Saint Jerome's staff. (The objects carried by saints in these pictures are always a great convenience to painters, who are free to tilt them this way and that for compositional reasons.)

There is nothing particularly original in the arrangement of this painting. Perugino is even notorious for the way he repeats his devices from picture to picture, reassembling them from a kind of stock pile. But he does satisfy beautifully the decorative demand for a painting that will not disturb the symmetry of an over-all scheme and the psychological demand for reverent peacefulness. There is even an agreeable clarity in the scheme's dependence upon the simplest and most apparent principles of arrangement. Virtually every element in the picture ties in with either the major or the secondary triangle or with the verticals —the cross, the towers, the delicate trees— that rise so quietly and so serenely upward.

## Picasso's Guernica

It would seem unlikely that anything having to do with a picture as quiet and simple as Perugino's *Crucifixion with Saints* could help us to understand a picture as violent and complicated as Picasso's *Guernica* (*Figure 6*), but compositionally the two paintings have an unexpected similarity. Perugino's altarpiece is a triptych, that is, it is made up of three separate panels, with each side panel measuring half the width of the central one. Picasso's

12

painting is not actually divided into panels, but it is also composed as a central scheme with two wings of half its width strongly divided from it by vertical lines, yet at the same time united to it, like Perugino's, by repeats and continuations of the main lines of a triangular formula. These the reader should be able to trace for himself.

*Guernica* is an extremely large painting, so large that one tends to look at it in sections. The triptychlike division makes the picture more satisfactory section by section; at the same time it affords a tightly knit composition when the picture is seen as a whole, as in our illustration, or at a sufficient distance from the original.

But all similarity between the two pictures ends with their compositional framework. Whereas Perugino is serene, Picasso is violent; whereas Perugino is content o be conventional, Picasso is explosively original. Perugino, through realism, creates an ideal beauty; Picasso, through abstraction, an expressive brutality.

Picasso's painting is an outraged indictment. During the Spanish revolution German bombers destroyed the city of Guernica in a practical experiment in mass bombing preliminary to the Second World War. The painting is a carnage of dead, dying, and mutilated animals and human beings. In the right "panel" a figure collapses in a flaming ruin On the left a bull, symbolizing brute force, rises triumphantly over a woman who shrieks in grief

*Figure* 7

13

*Figure 8*

(*Figure 7*) as she cradles her dead child. In the lower part of the central panel a severed arm holds a broken sword, the symbol of defeat. The head of the horse that rears from the center of the picture is grotesque, ugly, and, in a hideous way, ludicrous. But death by such violence is also grotesque, ugly, and even hideously ludicrous. *Guernica* is an overwhelming picture. There is every reason to believe that it will remain one of the masterpieces of our century.

Both Perugino's *Crucifixion* and Picasso's *Guernica* have as their subject social crimes of monstrous proportions. The difference is that the Perugino represents a social crime resolved into the divine blessing of man's salvation, and

hence it is painted with the serenity of divine significance. But nothing can resolve the crime of Guernica into anything better than a staggering demonstration of viciousness and brutality—hence it is painted in terms that are as ugly and as nightmarish as the crime itself.

## Composition
## in Three Dimensions

Having seen the foregoing examples, we should immediately recognize the triangular formula in Pollaiuolo's *Martyrdom of Saint Sebastian* (Plate 65). The executioners' bows and arrows define the scheme like direction pointers. The

14

arrows of the two men standing in the foreground point toward the apex of the triangle, while their bows, at right angles to the arrows, are part of the counter scheme, which is more conspicuously stated by the figures and arrows of the two bowmen in the center foreground.

But in this composition we have an important variation on the formula: here the composition demands to be read in depth, in three dimensions, if it is to be most effective. The executioners form a ring around the stake (*Figure 8*), and we read it as a ring. Thus, instead of a flat triangular composition we have what would be better described as a tent-shaped or cone-shaped or pyramidal composition. It is as if the flat triangle had been spun on its axis (the stake), and then all the forms had been arranged in the space thus defined. Pollaiuolo insists on the spatial character of his composition by the sweep of his landscape, which opens into space rather than hanging behind the bowmen like a tapestry on a wall.

He leads us into this depth by a series of transitions between the foreground, middleground, and background. A small plain with men and horses leads us to the river and hills into the horizon and the limitless depth of the sky. Admittedly the transition from foreground to middleground is rather abrupt. Dealing with the new concept of space in picturemaking, the painter was learning that the unification of foreground and background in three-dimensional compositions is one of the most vexing difficulties the painter has to solve.

Now it may be asked why painters developed an interest in three-dimensional space when the possibilities of two-dimensional expression are so great; it could even be argued that a painter is working on a two-dimensional surface and should respect it as such, leaving three-dimensional design to the sculptor, the architect, the stage designer, and any other artist whose medium legitimately and inevitably involves the third dimension. It may be asked why the Japanese and the Chinese, with their infinitely cultivated traditions in painting, never felt the necessity of creating spatial illusions but were content to express entire mountain ranges in a few washes upon a surface that was allowed to maintain its integrity.

A proper answer to these questions would require a volume of philosophical and historical explanation. But somewhere within it would be an examination of this point: that the Western scientific spirit, which insisted upon knowing the world by investigating its tangible realities, was born to all intents with the Italian Renaissance. Artists in harmony with their times were no longer content with pictorial symbols but sought instead to paint the world in images as nearly as possible real in a tangible sense. To this end they studied anatomy, invented perspective, and explored the laws of movement and light and color. It is obvious that objects drawn and painted to express a third dimension, to look solid, could not exist on a flat surface, hence this surface was "done away with" to create space in which solid objects could exist. When this happened the artist's problem as a pictorial composer ceased to be one of arranging flat shapes on a flat surface and became one of arranging space relationships between objects in depth.

We have just said that in *The Martyrdom of Saint Sebastian* Pollaiuolo was unable to make an entirely satisfactory transition from foreground to middle distance. He compromised by placing the foreground action upon some kind of ambiguous promontory that terminates—not satisfactorily, not quite understandably—and breaks the background in half.

## Composition in Space

How successfully this integration of space was finally achieved by later artists is apparent in Ruisdael's *Wheatfields* (Plate 66). The transition from foreground to infinity is easy and uninterrupted. As we enter the landscape and go deep into it space is all about us—beyond us, behind us, to every side, and infinitely above. Space is the dramatizing and unifying

*Figure 9*

component in this agreeable composition.

From the foreground, which we see as though we were standing upon a slight elevation, we are led down a road into a clump of trees, through them and into the vast cloud-filled sky. The trees, even though they partially obscure the horizon, are a zone to be entered and passed through, rather than a barrier. We are invited through natural alleyways between their trunks; we discover an area enclosed by an old wall, but it does not constitute an obstruction since we are faced by a wide opening (*Figure 9*).

As if to make certain that we feel free to enter and explore all this space, a man walks into the picture toward two figures in the middle distance, a woman holding a child by the hand. The forms of the landscape radiate around this pair like the spokes of a vast wheel around its hub, an effect emphasized by the outward lean of the trees at the right and of the dead branch in the left foreground.

There is nothing particularly unusual about the fields and objects making up this landscape, nor is there intended to be. It is a rather ordinary bit of countryside, even more ordinary to the people for whom it was painted than it is to us, since time has given the costumes a fillip of the quaint and foreign. Space, the place these objects occupy, the infinite depth to the horizon and beyond it, the infinite upward reach of the sky, is the artist's subject. The earth, the trees, the clouds, exist more to create this space than for their own inherent interest.

You may remember that in the first portfolio we compared two paintings, Cézanne's *Mont Sainte-Victoire* (Plate 8) and Durand's *Imaginary Landscape* (Plate 7), commenting that Durand sought to create limitless expanses stimulating to the imagination, while Cézanne sought the opposite, a contracted and enclosed landscape that could be comprehended by the intellect. These are the two basic approaches to spatial composition whether the subject is a landscape, a "roomscape" like the Vermeer of the artist's studio (Plate 37, Portfolio 4), or a figure composition. The picture we have just discussed, Ruisdael's *Wheatfields*, belongs in the same group as Durand's *Imaginary Landscape*. Of course it is a gentler, more realistic scene, but like the Durand it suggests that space is infinite, not defined, extending on every side beyond the limits of the frame. Vermeer's roomscape, on the contrary, kept us securely within a small, well-defined cube of space. The picture is satisfying; everything in it is so neatly disposed within defined space that a great sense of order, harmony, quiet, and security is relayed to us.

## Open Space and Closed Space

These two contrasting space conceptions can be called closed space and open space, or classical space and romantic space. As an example of a close-knit composition in classical space we will examine Piero della Francesca's *Madonna and Child with Saints and Angels Adored by Federigo da Montefeltro* (Plate 67), a formidable title for which we will substitute here the more convenient one of the Brera altarpiece, taking the name from the great gallery in Milan where the painting now hangs.

The Brera altarpiece is so important that we will approach it through an earlier painting, *Madonna of Mercy* (Plate 68), in which the artist is working toward the kind of spatial composition he so magnificently achieves in the later example. It would be a good idea to put the two illustrations side by side for comparison, making the most of an advantage open to us when we must study painting in reproduction instead of visiting the originals.

The *Madonna of Mercy* shows us the figure of Mary geometrized into a form approximating a channeled column surmounted by a head and neck of even more geometrical character. She extends her arms to make a shelter of her cape for the figures at her feet.

Considered in two dimensions it is an impressive painting; its air of contemplation and gravity is characteristic of all Piero's art. But as a composition in three dimensions its impressiveness is increased. The cape then forms a half-circle; we look into it as if it were a niche behind the columnlike figure. Seen in two dimensions the worshipers on either side are only rows of figures, but in three they form two half-circles into the depth of the picture, curving away from us into the niche of the robe. Thus the worshipful band surrounds the central figure instead of merely flanking it in clusters at either side.

This is a fairly elementary arrangement of forms, but in calling it elementary we must remember that Piero was a pioneer in three-dimensional composition. Also, the arrangement loses much of its three-dimensional effectiveness because the gold background is flat and tends to flatten the figures in front of it. Hence there is a contradiction between the three-dimensional arrangement of the figures and the flat background, a contradiction that could have been remedied by a background of painted forms harmonizing with the spatial forms in the foreground. Such a background could have repeated the columnlike and nichelike forms to emphasize instead of nullify them.

This is exactly what has been done in the Brera altarpiece. In this painting the artist amplifies the virtues and corrects the shortcomings of the *Madonna of Mercy*. The Brera altarpiece is completely three-dimensional in

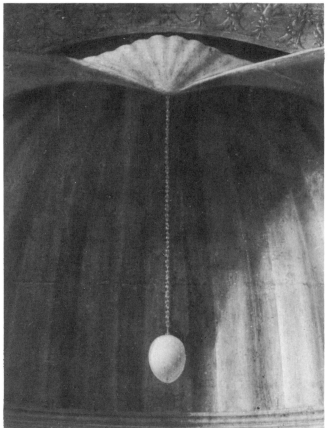

Photo by Alinari

*Figure 10*

back the form of a shell curves outward toward us. An egg (possibly a symbol of resurrection) suspended from the tip of the shell is the solid core of a series of spatial volumes surrounding it (*Figure 10*). These volumes are defined and enclosed by the projecting canopy, the niche, and the arch above it. Two other arches at the sides curve toward us, suggesting limitations of space instead of leaving us free to wander beyond this compact scene. If one figure breaks slightly from the scheme it is that of Federigo da Montefeltro, the armored man who kneels at the right. This divorce is intentional, for he alone among the congregation around the Madonna and Child is neither saint nor angel but merely the patron of the artist, and it is right that he should be a little separated from the holy band.

Compositionally the Brera altarpiece is so much an exercise in solid geometry that it is no surprise to learn that Piero della Francesca was as interested in mathematics as he was in painting. (He combined these interests to formulate the laws of perspective.) There are critics who feel that his late works, including the Brera altarpiece, are concerned too much with mathematics and too little with human sensitivities. Whether you agree or not will depend upon what you look for in painting. The Brera altarpiece has an extreme reserve, it is true, but for those who are sympathetic with Piero's analytical approach, the geometrical forms suggest a nobility and steadfastness that are appropriate in such a picture, lying beyond the too-human weaknesses and indecisions of the average person. This is expressed also in the curious grave facial type that Piero repeats again and again (*Figure 11*).

When we say that the quality of a painting like this one is architectonic we are not referring to the actual architectural elements like the niche and the arches that happen to be included in its composition. We mean that the scheme is conceived and arranged in terms of structure. In this case the creation of spatial volumes, a primary conception in real archi-

conception, so much so that if we analyze it as an arrangement of surface lines and shapes it is an indifferent composition—tending to divide into two parts, with its upper half occupied by an architectural background of some beauty but not much point.

But when the figures and background are regarded as a combination of solid objects and shaped space, the composition is tightly and beautifully unified in all its parts. *We have to remember that the voids, the space itself, are as important as the solid forms.* These voids are sometimes called negative volumes.

The various forms, positive or negative as volumes, combine to create an impression of majestic repose. Again the Madonna is encircled by saints and angels, but this time the ring spreads out in the foreground so that in a ground plan the figures would be standing in an arrangement like the letter omega ( ∩ ). The niche in the background is thoroughly integrated with this curving plan; from its

18

Photo by Alinari

*Figure 11*

19

*Figure 12*

tecture, does depend to a large extent upon the painted architecture in the picture, but the same architectonic attitude is present in the volumes created by the ring of figures, the egg, and the figures of the Madonna and Child.

## *"Architectonics" and Cézanne*

A painting like the Brera altarpiece that uses pictured architecture to create architectonic values may help us to understand the architectonic values in a painting like Cézanne's *The Card Players* (Plate 69), which does not. Cézanne made several versions of this subject, with varying numbers of figures, but all of them share the same solid and enduring quality so marked in this one. The direct comparison to architecture should not be pushed too far, but it is easy to see that the three men around the table suggest domelike space and the standing figure suggests the strength and stability of a column.

*The Card Players* lends itself to comparison

with architecture. And yet there is a significant human quality in this painting. Where does it come from and how does it manage to exist in harmony with abstract values like the architectonic forms we have been talking about? Why is the quality of human warmth present here, while it has been distilled out of the Brera altarpiece, which we analyzed in much the same compositional terms?

Cézanne's idea was that the fundamental dignity of human life, the fundamental order that

*Figure 13*

gives meaning to life, could be best expressed by geometrical forms of great solidity and simplicity arranged in organized space. In his paintings these forms are sometimes human beings, sometimes mountains, sometimes merely fruit and simple bowls and vases disposed on a table top. Ornate, precious, or unusual objects could have been used in the arrangements, but less successfully. Cézanne's importance as the father of modern abstract art is so great that too little attention is paid

20

to his subject matter. He may not be interested in his card players as personalities and he is not interested in them as members of a certain social class with certain problems; what is important in this picture is that the men are simple, earthy people (*Figures 12, 13, and 14*). One of them wears a peasant's smock. The picture might be almost—but not quite—as effective if the players were doctors, lawyers, or successful businessmen. Cézanne chooses to make them simple people for the same reason that he painted apples and pears in his still lifes instead of rare exotic fruits.

*The Card Players* is not first of all a picture of four honest men of an unpretentious social level. It is first of all a structure of solid shapes that interlock with spatial volumes. But it is wrong to argue that the subject matter has no importance at all. Many contemporary painters do so argue. They try to eliminate subject altogether, dealing with pure forms, as we saw in our discussion on abstraction. But Cézanne is one of the greatest painters in history be-

cause in pictures like *The Card Players* he has made such a perfect fusion of abstract and realistic values.

*The Card Players* was finished in 1892. It is difficult today, even for those who dislike modern art, to understand why Cézanne was so viciously attacked as an incompetent or degenerate painter. The figures in *The Card Players* look realistic in comparison with contemporary abstractions, but to the average person sixty years ago they looked appallingly crude. Popular taste demanded slicked-up, prettified, semiphotographic images. Even the more liberally educated art public regarded Renoir's portrait of his wife and Degas's *Woman with Chrysanthemums* (Plates 3 and 5, Portfolio 1) as examples of the kind of picture that had pushed modernism just about as far as it could go. As for the part played by the spatial structure of Cézanne's composition, it was beyond the understanding of more than a very few critics, and it is still the aspect of his art that is least recognized by a public that has learned to enjoy it.

Today students and critics have become preoccupied with spatial composition in modern art and in the art of old masters. It is the reason, in part, for the current revival of interest in the seventeenth-century painter Caravaggio, whose art, by the way, influenced Cézanne. *The Musicians* (Plate 70), seen side by side with Cézanne's *Card Players*, offers a variation in spatial composition reached from a similar point of departure. Both are composed of a main group of three closely related figures, with a fourth, subsidiary figure in the background. The Cézanne painting is powerful, the Caravaggio is elegant. The Cézanne is concerned with the basic values of human life, while the Caravaggio suggests cultivated ones. The Cézanne is simple in its final effect, the Caravaggio complicated.

Both pictures, however, are conceived as volumes within a block of space. The forms of the Caravaggio weave in and out, back and forth, carrying us into little pockets of space

*Figure 14*

21

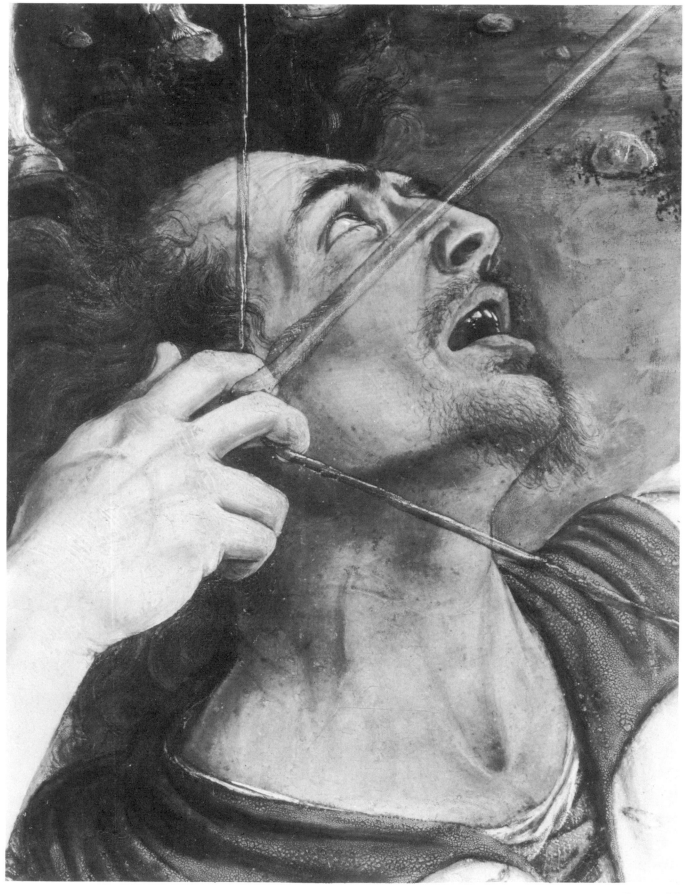

*Figure 15*

22

and leading us out of them, offering us a series of sensuous delights in the rich fabrics, fine woods, ripe fruit, and handsome youths.

The Cézanne, on the other hand, does not lead us from form to form but focuses on the completed structure as a whole. We may examine either picture detail by detail, of course, but our interest in the details of the Cézanne does not last long; it is the wonderful completeness that gives *The Card Players* its strength.

## Motion in Composition

The in-and-out movement of the Caravaggio suggests a new factor in composition—motion. Even the clashing forms of Picasso's *Guernica*, for all their violence, are held within an evenly balanced scheme; they are motionless, as if revealed in an instant of blinding illumination. Pollaiuolo's *Martyrdom of Saint Sebastian*, which also illustrates a subject of some violence, is without movement. The archers are frozen at the precise moment when they are about to release their arrows (*Figure 15*) or just about to complete the action of reloading their bows. We have commented on the wave of action in Leonardo's *Last Supper*, but the wave passes along a series of essentially static forms and does not go into the depth of the picture. The Caravaggio has something of this same flowing quality except that, as we have seen, the flow is into and out of and around and about rather than across the surface as in the case of *The Last Supper*. The musicians are not actually in motion, but the sinuous lines, which keep the eye moving within the picture, suggest motion.

When a painter deals with a subject of violent motion he must adapt his composition to express it. How one painter solved the problem of composing a picture that is at once a structure and an expression of violent motion is demonstrated in Géricault's *The Raft of the Medusa* (Plate 71), where the survivors of a shipwreck are crowded on a raft in a stormy sea with others who are dead and dying. The picture rushes upward from the lower left to the upper right, where the figure of a young man, supported by a struggling group, waves in an attempt to attract the attention of a ship in the distance.

It is at once apparent that again we have a composition that builds up to a climactic figure by means of a triangle. The usual devices of outstretched arms, the direction of some glances, the disposition of draperies—all these play their conventional roles. The difference is that the triangle is pushed off center so that it leans far to the right side instead of resting in the center of the picture. This un-balance does not constitute action in the literal sense of the word, but this composition creates the effect of action. You need only imagine the climactic figure at the top of a symmetrical triangle, centered in the space, to see that the effect of motion would be lost or reduced, no matter how much the individual figures writhed and twisted in an attempt to create movement.

This off-centered triangle leaves the picture overweighted on one side. Géricault brings it back into balance by creating a second triangle leaning in the opposite diagonal direction. The mast of the raft and the two ropes that support it define this counter triangle. It is a strong form, but since inanimate objects are inherently less interesting than human figures, the triangle of massed survivors continues to hold our interest against the strong counter action. But to make certain that they do, the artist has weakened the counter triangle and strengthened the main one by a simple device: he interrupts the strongest line of the counter triangle by cutting the line of the rope against the sky by an arm that points toward the peak of the main triangle.

The result is a composition that creates an effect of action by its off-balance climax, but retains its strength as a pictorial structure by a neat counterbalance. And the whole scheme is a variation of a fundamental formula that had been effective in one treatment or

*Figure 16*

another for at least several hundred years.

*The Raft of the Medusa* is a conspicuous landmark in the history of painting because it became a battle cry for the famous romantic movement, which stressed emotionalism and individual invention instead of the intellectualism and convention that dominated painting at the time. We have already made the distinction between classical space, or closed space, and romantic space. Actually, although *The Raft of the Medusa* is played against a far horizon, it does not unite the figures with space. They are arranged like a monument against a distant horizon. A later romantic picture, Delacroix's *The Abduction of Rebecca* (Plate 72), is a fuller expression of romantic composition.

The Delacroix swirls from the foreground deep into the background, from the cyclonic forms of the horse, the abductors, and the victim to the excitement around the burning fortress, so that the principal figures are not only played against depth but also integrated with it. Can we analyze the tempestuous forms of the main group? Not with the same-clarity as in our earlier, more static compositions. But we can see that the excitement raging is expressed by the constant turns, reversals, and interruptions of forms and their directions. The rider twists backward into the picture, while the figure of Rebecca is thrust forward toward us. The horse is ready to charge in a third direction, and the rider's head is turned in the opposite one. Through the whole group lines snake and twist without rest. Color explodes in fragments over the turbulent forms.

This fragmented color is in direct opposition to the decisively confined color areas of Poussin's *Rape of the Sabine Women*, to which we are now ready to return. Several questions arise in the light of what has been said since we saw it first. Is it a composition in three-dimensional space? We analyzed its framework in two dimensions across its surface. What about the emotionalism of the subject and the apparently contradictory controlled definition of the arrangement? What about

this static composition for a subject of such violent action?

The thing to remember about the Poussin is that it is in no sense an illustration nor is it an emotionalized expression. It is an intellectual synthesis devoted to the classical ideal of ultimate clarity.

The depth of the Poussin is a defined block of static space like that of the Cézanne and the Caravaggio, rather than a portion of swirling limitless space as in the Delacroix. The figures don't seem to move (*Figure 16*), as Delacroix's do; their passion, terror, and rage are not emotionalized for the observer, but objectified. We do not participate in the abduction of the Sabine women as we do in the abduction of Rebecca. Instead of participating, we contemplate; instead of feeling, we reflect; instead of being in a world of action and conflict we are in a world where all indecisions have been resolved. This is the classical world, where order has been imposed upon chaos, and to some temperaments it will always seem too static, a little cold, and impossible of reconciliation with violence. But for others there is more satisfaction in this harmoniously disposed world of Poussin, a world of complex balances and multiple relationships distilled from human experience. Poussin's composition says that all human experience is meaningful beyond its moment, that the moment may be overpowering in the immediacy of its joy or anguish, but that there is an eternal order within which the moment is absorbed.

We have been discussing composition in this portfolio as if all pictures could be reduced to some compositional formula. Many can. The pictures we have explained were chosen because they are variations of a few general types or formulas you will find in other variations by the hundreds.

But some of the greatest compositions in the world fall into no type or group because they are uniquely appropriate to a single painting and invented for it. Our next portfolio examines a few of them.

# Notes on the Painters

Photo by Anderson

## Leonardo da Vinci, 1452-1519, Italian

### 61. THE LAST SUPPER, 1495-98

*Oil tempera on plaster. Height 13'9¼". Refectory of the Monastery of Santa Maria delle Grazie, Milan*

In painting *The Last Supper* Leonardo applied an experimental emulsion directly on the refectory wall, and even during his lifetime the picture had begun to disintegrate. Since then it has not only been neglected but abused. It has been repainted—the worst thing, short of total destruction, that can happen to any picture. At one time a doorway was knocked through the lower part of it. For a while the refectory was used as a stable. During the Second World War the building was partially destroyed, and behind layers of protective sandbags *The Last Supper* mildewed badly. These misfortunes have been alleviated from time to time by judicious efforts at restoration and preservation, but we will never be sure that we are seeing anything but an approximation of Leonardo's great work—except in the lines of its composition.

When the sandbags were removed after the recent disaster, *The Last Supper* was in such pitiful condition that historians were ready to list it as a war casualty. But since then the entire picture has been gone over as definitively as the combination of exhaustive scholarship and high technical skill make possible to preserve once and for all whatever is discoverable of the original work. The results are better than anyone expected, although the painting still suggests a ghost at best or, at worst, an embalmed relic. The new building and the attendant museum exhibits now surrounding *The Last Supper* increase the rather chilling impression that this is not a picture to which we can respond, but an important curiosity that we may examine upon payment of a moderate fee.

In the discussion of Leonardo's *Mona Lisa* in Portfolio 1, the point was made that the picture is hard to judge because one never comes upon it as if for the first time; it has become more an institution than a work of art. *The Last Supper* struggles under something of the same limitation, plus a worse one. It has been so debased in countless saccharine copies that even when we are in its presence the original appears deformed.

(Other comments on Leonardo are included in the Notes, Portfolio 1.)

Photo by Anderson

## Raphael, 1483-1520, Italian

### 62. THE TRANSFIGURATION, 1517-20

*Oil on canvas. Height 13'1½". The Vatican, Rome*

Raphael's portrait *Giuliano de' Medici, Duke of Nemours* was included in the second portfolio of this series with comments on the nicety of its compositional arrangement. Raphael was, in fact, a master of composition, to such a degree that his reputation can well afford the reservations made here concerning *The Transfiguration*. By the end of his life Raphael's typically serene style was being affected by the violence of Michelangelo's innovations. *The Transfiguration* was in part an unsuccessful effort to assimilate them. It was finished after his death by his favorite pupil and assistant, Giulio Romano (1499-1546), but it is not likely that the picture's composition was much changed by this rather heavy-handed painter.

## Nicolas Poussin, 1593/94-1665, French

### 63. THE RAPE OF THE SABINE WOMEN, BEFORE 1637

*Oil on canvas. Height 60⅞". The Metropolitan Museum of Art, Dick Fund, 1946*

When all is said, Poussin is probably the most generally revered of all painters, at least by his countrymen. Even painters who work at the wildest extremes in other directions reflect him. Even cubism owes a debt to him. Cézanne, the father of modern painting, said, "I want to do Poussin over again, after nature," meaning that he wanted to emulate the classical perfection of Poussin's pictorial organization, but in terms of the daily world. *The Card Players* does so. Its structure is as monumental and as static as Poussin's, as architectonic in quality, and yet in contrast with Poussin's austere impersonality the picture is full of human warmth.

Comments made heretofore on the art of the seventeenth century—Poussin's century—have concerned baroque realism, with its emphasis upon sensation. But in the complex web of the arts, no period is purely one thing or another, and the seventeenth-century baroque spirit also had its classical manifestation. Poussin is this manifestation in painting, although like any artist of absolutely first rank he need not be associated with his time to be understood in his most profound meaning.

During his lifetime Poussin was only moderately successful—moderately, that is, in comparison with his near-deification in historical retrospect. His popularity was limited to a small group who understood his intellectual magnitude and a larger one who enjoyed his classical references without grasping their deeper implications. He worked largely in Italy, and his major influence from the past came from Raphael and Raphael's serene organization of classically derived forms.

Poussin is further considered in the next portfolio, where his landscape *The Funeral of Phocion* is analyzed.

## Pietro Perugino, 1445-1523, Italian

### 64. CRUCIFIXION WITH SAINTS, ABOUT 1485

*Oil and tempera transferred from wood to canvas. Height 39⅞". The National Gallery of Art, Washington, Mellon Collection*

The most obvious characteristics of the best work of Perugino, a painter of the Umbrian school, are the sweetness and grace apparent in his altarpiece *Crucifixion with Saints*. In his routine paintings Perugino could be shallow and sickly.

The Umbrians made an important contribution to the development of painting by their sensitivity to landscape. The limpid skies, gentle formations of hills and rocks, delicate trees, and serene rivers are lucidly combined in deep space to form the backgrounds for Umbrian paintings. In their poetic feeling they prefigure later developments when landscape becomes an independent theme rather than an accessory to a subject picture. Its most lyrical expression in Umbrian painting is found in the earliest work of Perugino's pupil Raphael, before he went to the greater centers of art, Florence and Rome. The spatial implications of these deep landscapes were developed in the art of Piero della Francesca, who was Umbrian by birth and remains so by classification though he was Florentine in the austerity, vigor, and intellectual calculation of his art.

Perugino also worked in Florence and Rome, executing one of his finest works in fresco on the walls of the Sistine Chapel (which play second fiddle to Michelangelo's ceiling) and decorating the ceiling of a room in the Vatican where his former student, Raphael, did the important frescoes on the walls. If all of this makes Perugino sound like an also-ran, the impression is false. He achieved a major reputation, prospered (gaining a certain reputation in the history books as a money-grubber), and lived into his seventies, contentedly repeating and recombining elements from earlier pictures, though his manner was by then outmoded by the grander forms of the High Renaissance.

## Antonio Pollaiuolo, 1432-1498, Italian

### 65. THE MARTYRDOM OF SAINT SEBASTIAN, FINISHED IN 1475

*Oil and tempera on wood. Height 9'6". The National Gallery, London*

Pollaiuolo was one of the most devoted investigators among the early Florentine painters who explored the natural world around them with an enthusiasm unequaled before the birth of modern laboratory techniques. His passion was the anatomy of the human body, the construction of muscles upon the bones, and the action of these muscles as the body moved. His hard-bitten, fiercely realistic figures make no concessions to grace or prettiness.

Everywhere this preoccupation with the form of the body is apparent. In *The Martyrdom of Saint Sebastian* we come close to an anatomical demonstration piece. The two archers in the center in the immediate foreground are front and back views of the same figure, analyzed as the action of a muscular body straining at its task. The bowmen at the extreme left and right are a similar pair. Pollaiuolo's drawings of nudes (and these figures were certainly first drawn as nudes, a usual practice) are, in their harsh way, among the most beautiful in the history of draughtsmanship.

But his drawing—and his painting—is far more than a mere record of his study of muscles and their disposition in action. He is an artist and a designer, not a scientist. Hence, his intensely observed descriptions of form are resolved into contours whose linear boundaries are beautiful in themselves. The right leg of the foremost bowman can serve as a clear example. Not beautiful as a leg, anatomically accurate (with some exaggeration), hard as stone, it is still beautiful as a drawing.

Antonio's brother Piero collaborated with him, particularly in sculpture. The brothers were goldsmiths as well, at a time when the craft produced objects of the most extreme elaboration. The finely wrought, decisive character of early Florentine goldsmith work is reflected in Antonio's painting and even more strongly in the single engraving known to be by him. This single print, however, puts him in the front rank of engravers. In it ten nude men battle with swords against a friezelike background of tree and vine forms. From one branch hangs a tablet upon which Antonio has signed his name, followed by the proud word *Florentini* (the Florentine). And indeed of all early Florentine painters Antonio might best stand as representative of his generation in the vigor, the passionate curiosity, the uncompromising technical skill, and the fascination with the classical past that characterize his work. This last is evident in the architectural fragment at the left in *The Martyrdom of Saint Sebastian*. Antonio also did numerous paintings of classical subjects.

Antonio Pollaiuolo's linear design and expressiveness find a gentler echo in the art of a younger painter, Sandro Botticelli, whose *La Primavera* was discussed in Portfolio 5. The use of figures ranged against a backdrop of ornamental foliage in *La Primavera* draws upon Antonio's great engraving *The Battle of the Naked Men* (illustrated in Portfolio 10).

## Jacob Isaacksz. van Ruisdael, 1628/29-1682, Dutch

66. WHEATFIELDS

   *Oil on canvas. Height 39⅜". The Metropolitan Museum of Art, bequest of Benjamin Altman, 1913*

Ruisdael, or Ruysdael, was a student of his uncle, Salomon van Ruysdael. Although Holland already had a flourishing school of landscape painters, of whom Salomon was one, Jacob expanded this minor art into a major one. *Wheatfields* is one of his finest achievements, exemplifying his feeling for the grandeur of space and his lyrical feeling for the everyday world of nature. But he is equally successful in depicting other moods through landscape—moods of romantic mystery and melancholy in pictures filled with thunderous skies, rough crags, dark torrents, or cemeteries where tombstones emerge from encroaching foliage into sudden spectral lights.

## Piero della Francesca, about 1420-1492, Italian

67. MADONNA AND CHILD WITH SAINTS AND ANGELS ADORED BY FEDERIGO DA MONTEFELTRO, 1474-78 (?)

   *Tempera on wood. Height 8'2". The Brera Gallery, Milan*

68. MADONNA OF MERCY, center panel, 1445-55

   *Oil and tempera on wood. Height about 57". The Communal Palace, Borgo San Sepolcro*

Photo by Alinari

Piero was considered in Portfolio 4 in the discussion of abstraction. A few decades ago he would have been found listed in art history books as a minor painter with a highly individual style. During his own lifetime he never worked in the great centers of painting and therefore exerted less influence than he might have in Florence or Rome. But it would be difficult to find a serious painter or critic today who would place him anywhere but in the very top bracket of the greatest painters of the Renaissance. The present recognition of his stature is of course partly the result of the contemporary painter's study of space and volume as abstract constants in art.

## Paul Cézanne, 1839-1906, French

69. THE CARD PLAYERS, 1890-92

   *Oil on canvas. Height 25⅝". Stephen C. Clark, New York*

Cézanne also appears for the second time in the Seminars, having been contrasted with a romantic landscapist in the first portfolio. His analysis of form and space, recognized as the very cornerstone of modern art, was one

Photo by Anderson

of the "back doors" that led to the re-evaluation of Piero della Francesca's art. Although the two men bear virtually no superficial resemblances to one another, both based their art on spatial analysis. Piero was concerned with the then new science of perspective as a point of departure, while Cézanne abandoned conventional perspective for new theories he sought to develop for himself. Thus their means differed, but their end was the same, to create monumental expressions through monumental forms.

## Michelangelo Merisi da Caravaggio, 1573-1610, Italian

### 70. THE MUSICIANS, 1594-95

*Oil on canvas. Height 36¼". The Metropolitan Museum of Art, Rogers Fund, 1952*

Caravaggio appeared at a time when the noble style of the High Renaissance was desiccating into affectation and pedantry. He studied under obscure masters of little originality, but he prodigiously developed his own unprecedented dramatic realism, which was to determine the major direction of Italian painting for the following century. To a small degree, but to a degree still unique in the Renaissance, which was usually sympathetic to revolutionary developments in the arts, Caravaggio suffered for his originality. His saints, biblical characters, and even his angels and his Christs had an earthiness appalling to the art patrons of the day, particularly to the Church. But Caravaggio found partisans as enthusiastic as his detractors were outraged. In a very short lifetime, in which he found plenty of time for brawling, he produced an extraordinary number of important pictures. His historical significance is that he turned the current of painting away from formulated intellectualism, or semi-intellectualism, toward the most direct reference to the ordinary world. His religious pictures are enacted by common people who respond as human beings to the miraculous situations in which they find themselves. Caravaggio stages these *tableaux vivants* in an exaggerated, theatrical chiaroscuro (light and shade) that intensified their statement for the next generation of painters, who discovered that their century had to accept miracles in terms of human, rather than divine, experience. The baroque realism fathered by Caravaggio was discussed earlier in connection with two paintings by Rubens, his *Prometheus Bound* (Plate 18, Portfolio 2) and his *Christ on the Cross* (Plate 33, Portfolio 3).

In his nonreligious paintings, like *The Musicians*, Caravaggio's realism takes the form of sensuous presentation of handsome youths surrounded with luxurious stuffs, a luscious paganism presented in terms as concrete as those of his worldly dramatization of mystical stories.

Photo by Archives Photographiques, Paris

## Jean Louis André Théodore Géricault, 1791-1824, French

### 71. THE RAFT OF THE MEDUSA, 1818

*Oil on canvas. Height 16'1". The Louvre Museum, Paris*

Géricault, coming two centuries after Caravaggio, found himself in a similar situation. In a lifetime also of short duration, thirty-three years, he created something of the same furor and had, in a much smaller way, the same influence on the course of painting. When Géricault began painting, French art was dominated by the classicism of the official academic painters. Géricault rejected the rather frigid idealism of classicism in favor of romantic passion expressed in realistic images. Some of the figures in *The Raft of the*